SOLVING the MYSTERIES of the PAST

GERARD AKSOMITIS

Crabtree Publishing Company

www.crabtreebooks.com

Crabtree Publishing Company
www.crabtreebooks.com

Author: Gerard Aksomitis
Project editor: Tom Jackson
Designer: Lynne Lennon
Picture researcher: Sophie Mortimer
Indexer: Kay Ollerenshaw
Managing editor: Miranda Smith
Art director: Jeni Child
Design manager: David Poole
Editorial director: Lindsey Lowe
Children's publisher: Anne O'Daly
Editor: Adrianna Morganelli
Proofreaders: Michael Hodge, Crystal Sikkens
Project coordinator: Robert Walker
Production coordinator: Katherine Kantor
Font management: Mike Golka
Prepress technician: Katherine Kantor

This edition published in 2009 by
Crabtree Publishing Company.

The Brown Reference Group plc,
First Floor, 9–17 St. Albans Place,
London, N1 0NX
www.brownreference.com

Copyright © 2009 The Brown Reference Group plc

Photographs:
BRG: p. 27 (bottom)
Corbis: Yann Arthus-Bertrand: p. 9 (top); Christophe Boisvieux:
p. 18 (bottom), 22 (top); Robert Essel NYC: p. 18–19; Muzzi
Fabio/Sygma: p. 12-13; Les Stone/Sygma: p. 13 (top), 14 (left);
Charles O'Rear: p. 20–21; Reuters: p. 7 (bottom); Remigiusz
Sikora/epa: p. 11
NASA: p. 6 (bottom), 9 (bottom)
Science Photo Library: Michael Donne, University of Manchester:
p. 21 (bottom); Equinox Graphics: p. 28–29; Mauro
Fermariello: p. 19 (bottom), 20 (bottom); James King-Holmes:
p. 16 (left); Patrick Landmann: p. 23; Philippe Psaila: p. 8; John
Reader: p. 29; Alexis Rosendfeld: p. 7 (top); Silkeborg Museum
Denmark/Munoz-Yague: p. 15 (top); Sheila Terry: p. 22 (bottom)
Shutterstock: Kharidehal Abhirama Ashwin: cover; Bob Ainsworth:
p. 26 (left); Alistair Michael Thomas: p. 5 (bottom); alliciahh: p. 24
(bottom); Joseph Calev: p. 14 (bottom right); Pablo H. Caridad:
p. 28 (left); Cristina Ciochina: p. 25 (bottom); Jarno Gonzalez:
p. 10 (bottom); Vladimir Korostyshevdkiy: p. 4–5; Jane McIlroy:
p. 15 (bottom); Lisa Mcknown: p. 16 (right); Nicholas Moore:
p. 10 (right); Kenneth V. Pilon: p. 13 (bottom), 17; E. G. Pors:
p. 25 (top); Styve Reineck: p. 24–25; topal: p. 6–7, 10 (left)
Topfoto: Bob Daemmrichr/Image Works: p. 26 (right)

Every effort has been made to trace the owners of
copyrighted material.

Library and Archives Canada Cataloguing in Publication

Aksomitis, Gerard
    Solving the mysteries of the past / Gerard Aksomitis.

(Science solves it)
Includes index.
ISBN 978-0-7787-4171-8 (bound).–ISBN 978-0-7787-4178-7 (pbk.)

    1. Archaeology–Juvenile literature. 2. Antiquities–Juvenile literature.
3. Excavations (Archaeology)–Juvenile literature. 4. Archaeologists–
Juvenile literature. I. Title. II. Series: Science solves it (St. Catharines, Ont.)

CC171.A38 2008   j930.1   C2008-905012-6

Library of Congress Cataloging-in-Publication Data

Aksomitis, Gerard.
    Solving the mysteries of the past / Gerard Aksomitis.
        p. cm. – (Science solves it)
Includes index.
    ISBN-13: 978-0-7787-4178-7 (pbk. : alk. paper)
    ISBN-10: 0-7787-4178-8 (pbk. : alk. paper)
    ISBN-13: 978-0-7787-4171-8 (reinforced lib. bdg. : alk. paper)
    ISBN-10: 0-7787-4171-0 (reinforced lib. bdg. : alk. paper)
    1. Archaeology–Juvenile literature. 2. Antiquities–Juvenile literature. 3.
Excavations (Archaeology)–Juvenile literature. 4. Archaeologists–Juvenile
literature. I. Title.
    CC171.A47 2009
    930.1–dc22
                                          2008033790

Crabtree Publishing Company
www.crabtreebooks.com   1-800-387-7650

**Published in Canada
Crabtree Publishing**
616 Welland Ave.
St. Catharines, ON
L2M 5V6

**Published in the United States
Crabtree Publishing**
PMB 59051
350 Fifth Ave., 59th Floor
New York, NY 10118

Printed in the USA/012014/CG20131129

CONTENTS

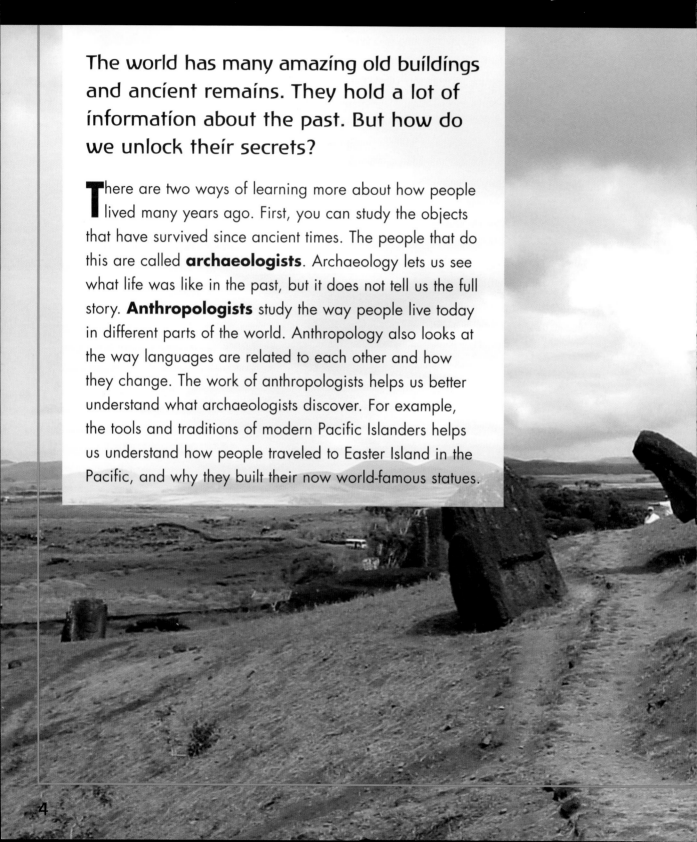

DIGGING FOR HISTORY

The world has many amazing old buildings and ancient remains. They hold a lot of information about the past. But how do we unlock their secrets?

There are two ways of learning more about how people lived many years ago. First, you can study the objects that have survived since ancient times. The people that do this are called **archaeologists**. Archaeology lets us see what life was like in the past, but it does not tell us the full story. **Anthropologists** study the way people live today in different parts of the world. Anthropology also looks at the way languages are related to each other and how they change. The work of anthropologists helps us better understand what archaeologists discover. For example, the tools and traditions of modern Pacific Islanders helps us understand how people traveled to Easter Island in the Pacific, and why they built their now world-famous statues.

Easter Island is the most remote island on Earth. It has 800 mysterious stone heads made about 1,000 years ago. No one is quite sure why they are there— perhaps they are the heads of important island chiefs.

BECOMING AN ARCHAEOLOGIST

Do you think you would like to become an archaeologist? Archaeologists spend a lot of time in school. They also learn on the job. Most choose to become experts in one ancient period. Archaeologists work at "digs" to uncover ancient objects. They look for coins, pottery, walls, fireplaces, and other things people made many years ago. Most archaeologists do not dig all year around. Their other work might include running a museum or teaching at a college.

ON A DIG

The first archaeologists did not have much training. Today, archaeologists learn how to work carefully and thoroughly.

Archaeological fieldwork is much more complicated now than in the past. Archaeologists make sure they do not damage an ancient site. Some dig sites, like those under water, also require special equipment.

LOOKING FROM SPACE

In 1981, NASA launched a satellite for studying Earth's surface. The satellite does not make pictures using light. Instead, it uses **radar** — radio waves that are echoed off of Earth. The satellite makes images from the echoes. Radar pictures of the Sahara Desert in Africa revealed ancient riverbeds in the sand. Archaeologists use radar images to find similar ancient features to investigate.

LOOK UNDER WATER

French archaeologist Franck Goddio is a world leader in underwater archaeology. Goddio helped set up two major research centers for digging through remains under water. Franck has also discovered 14 sunken ships and several long forgotten underwater cities.

Everything you find at a dig is important—even if it is broken, it tells us about life in the past.

GRAVE CONCERNS

Clea Koff is a **forensic** anthropologist. She worked in Rwanda, where many people were killed in a war in the 1990s. Clea studied graves in the country. She figured out from the dead bodies how they were killed and whether they were soldiers or regular people.

WHERE TO DIG?

Archaeology began in the 19th century, when Europeans began to dig through ancient ruins looking for treasure. In those days it was quite easy to find a good place to dig—they looked for old buildings in Greece, Egypt, and in other places in the Mediterranean and Middle East.

Today, archaeologists use advanced **technology** to find ancient sites that are hidden from view. **Aerial** photography highlights features that are not visible from the ground.

UNDERWATER SEARCH

Many of the latest dig sites are in harsh places, such as deserts or even under the sea. Archaeologists use the latest technology to work in these tough conditions. The first underwater archaeologists dove to the seabed holding their breath and hauled objects back to surface. Today, researchers can dive deeper and for longer thanks to **aqualungs** and **submersibles**. However, they leave most of what they find in place and make detailed plans instead.

UNDERWATER CITY

Alexandria is a port at the mouth of the Nile River, in Egypt, Africa. It was founded by Alexander the Great in 332 B.C. and was the home of Cleopatra. However, by 1,600 years ago, sea levels had risen, and ancient Alexandria was covered in water. In 1996, Franck Goddio (below) rediscovered the remains on the seabed using radar probes and remote-controlled submersibles. There are now maps of the underwater parts of the city.

The Nazca Lines are giant drawings cut into a rocky desert in Peru, South America. They were made about 2,000 years ago. Nobody is sure why. They would have been hard to see until the invention of airplanes in the early 20th century.

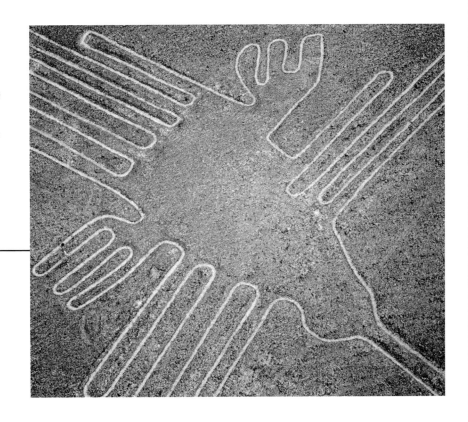

A CITY SWALLOWED BY SAND

The first aerial photos were taken in the 1900s once aircraft had become reliable. The pictures were useful for archaeologists. For example, they showed the mounds and ditches that were once part of ancient castles and villages. Satellite photos have also become a powerful tool. In 1992, researchers used a satellite image (left) to find the lost city of Ubar in Oman in the Middle East. The city was once a large port, but 1,700 years ago, a huge cavern beneath Ubar collapsed. The city sunk into the hole and was swallowed by the sand.

VISITING THE PAST

Scientists have found traces left by ancient people all over the world. Graves and **middens** are two of the most common finds. Middens are garbage dumps that have been **preserved**. They are a good thing to find because archaeologists can learn a lot from what people have thrown away.

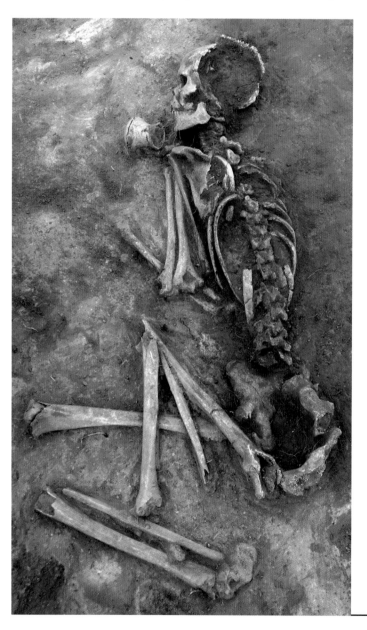

EXAMINE THE FACTS

You can study your own midden by looking in your family's trash can. Empty the garbage and make a list of the items. What can you learn from them? For example, printed or written records can tell you a lot, such as how old a person is and what they are interested in.

Ancient people were not always buried in caskets. Instead, they were laid to rest in a curled position. Ancient graves from all over the world show that people always treated dead bodies with great respect, just as we do now.

WHO'S THE MUMMY?

Egypt has some well-known gravesites. The most famous are the Pyramids, and many **tombs** contain mummies— bodies preserved in cloth. Anthropologists use **X-ray** scanners from hospitals to look inside the mummies. The remains inside tell them about how people lived in ancient Egypt—what they ate, how healthy they were, and when they died.

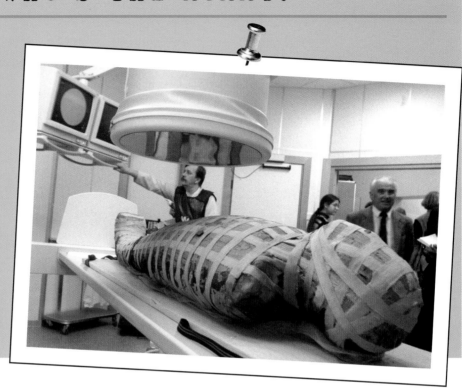

Middens contain a lot of leftover food. That shows us what the kinds of **diets** people had and how they prepared food. Middens also show how long people stayed in one place— whether it was a permanent town or just a camp. Any metal and clay objects show the skills of ancient craftspeople.

THE DEAD TELL A STORY

Graves give archaeologists information about the past, as well. Even if the body has **decayed**, ancient graves often contain grave goods. Grave goods are items buried along with a body. The goods tell archaeologists a lot about the person in the grave. Chiefs were buried with gold and jewels, while warriors often have their weapons by their side. All this helps to build a picture of life in the past.

Grave goods are items buried along with a body. They help an archaeologist understand ancient life.

Ancient **artifacts** have survived for centuries, and can often be very fragile. Studying them requires a lot of care.

Scientists look for new ways to find information from ancient objects without destroying them. Chemists **analyze** the substances in an object to figure out how old it is. Once scientists know the age of one item, they can use it to date others found near it. For example, another artifact buried underneath the already dated item is probably older.

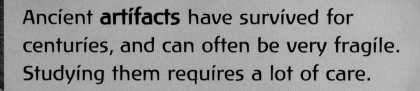

Everything found at a dig is recorded, showing when and where it was found.

PRESERVING BODIES

When it comes to preserving **mummified** bodies, there are many different ways to do it. Juanita the Ice Maiden is a 500-year-old girl found frozen on Mount Ampato, in Peru, South America. Today Juanita is in deep-freeze in a museum. Other frozen bodies and **cairns** (right) have been found near Juanita's grave.

SECRET SCROLLS

Father Guerin de Vaux was a French priest. He was the lead researcher investigating the Dead Sea Scrolls—documents written more than 2,000 years ago in the Middle East. De Vaux made the investigation into the documents a secret.

TURIN SHROUD

In 1355, the French de Charny family put the Shroud of Turin on display for the first time. The shroud shows the face and body of a man said to be Jesus Christ.

REAL LIFE

For about 40 years after they were discovered the Dead Sea Scrolls were kept secret. However, in the 1990s all the documents were made public. Most of them were in thousands of pieces (below) and no one knew what they said. Scientists have developed a computer program to recognize the words and fit the pieces together.

SECRET SCROLLS

A lot of archaeology takes place in labs. There, researchers figure out the histories of different objects. They then put these together to build a detailed picture of life in the distant past.

Some discoveries can change the way we understand history. For example, the Dead Sea Scrolls, found in 1947, contain religious writings from about 2,100 years ago. Some people think the scrolls come from an ancient library in Jerusalem.

The Dead Sea Scrolls were found in eleven caves along the shore of the Dead Sea. The **papyrus** scrolls were stored in clay jars and they were preserved by the dry desert air.

SWAMP THINGS

Many bodies have been found in **peat bogs**. The damp, airless conditions in the peat stopped the bodies from decaying. Many of these "bogmen" did not die of natural causes. They were killed and then thrown into the bog. Their stomach contents shows us that many victims had eaten special meals before they died. This makes it likely that they were killed as part of a religious ceremony.

Tollund Man lay in a bog in Denmark, Europe, for 2,400 years.

BOGMEN OF IRELAND

Clonycavan Man and Oldcroghan Man were dug up from bogs in Ireland (right). Their bodies show us what life was like in the **Iron Age**. Clonycavan was 5 foot 2 inches (157 cm) tall. He used a hair gel made from plant oils to make his hair stick up. The oil in the gel was traced to Spain. Oldcroghan was a giant at 6 foot 6 inches (256 cm) tall. He had neat fingernails. This tells us he did not have to work and was a high-ranking member of society.

WHAT'S THE DATE?

Radiocarbon dating is a way of telling how old an object is. It only works on things that are made from materials that came originally from animals or plants. When something is alive, the amount of **radioactive** carbon in it stays the same. Once it dies, the level slowly drops over hundreds of years. Scientists measure the level of carbon in the object, which tells them exactly how old it is.

HALF-LIFE

Half-life is the amount of time it takes for half of the **atoms** in a radioactive substance to break up. The half-life for a particular substance is always the same. Radioactive carbon has a half-life of 5,730 years.

Radiocarbon dating needs only a small test sample.

BACK IN TIME

Radiocarbon dating can pinpoint the year that an artifact was made, up to 50,000 years ago. Being able to date objects so accurately has had a big effect on our understanding of human history. In 1960, American scientist Willard F. Libby was awarded the **Nobel Prize** for Chemistry for inventing the process.

Scientists measure the level of carbon in the object, which tells them exactly how old it is.

TURIN SHROUD

The Shroud of Turin is one of the most famous artifacts in history. Many people claim the shroud is a fake. Others maintain that the cloth shows the face of Jesus. Radiocarbon dating showed that the shroud was made in the 1300s—about the time it was first shown in public. However, some scientists point out that the sample dated was from a repair done in the **Middle Ages**. The debate continues.

We can learn about the past by studying the way people live today. The many different **cultures** of the world show us how ancient people might have lived.

Anthropologists have a variety of tools for linking the past to the present. They rebuild the homes and communities of ancient people to figure out what it was like to live at that time. **Genetic** testing is used to trace the **migration** of people. Forensic artists are able to reconstruct the faces and bodies of dead people.

TESTING IDEAS

Thor Heyerdahl of Norway decided to find out if it was possible to use ancient technology to travel across the world. He made several voyages, crossing the Pacific Ocean in a wooden raft (right) and sailing the Atlantic in a ship made from bundles of reeds. Heyerdahl's voyages offered a new way of thinking about the routes ancient peoples took as they spread across the world.

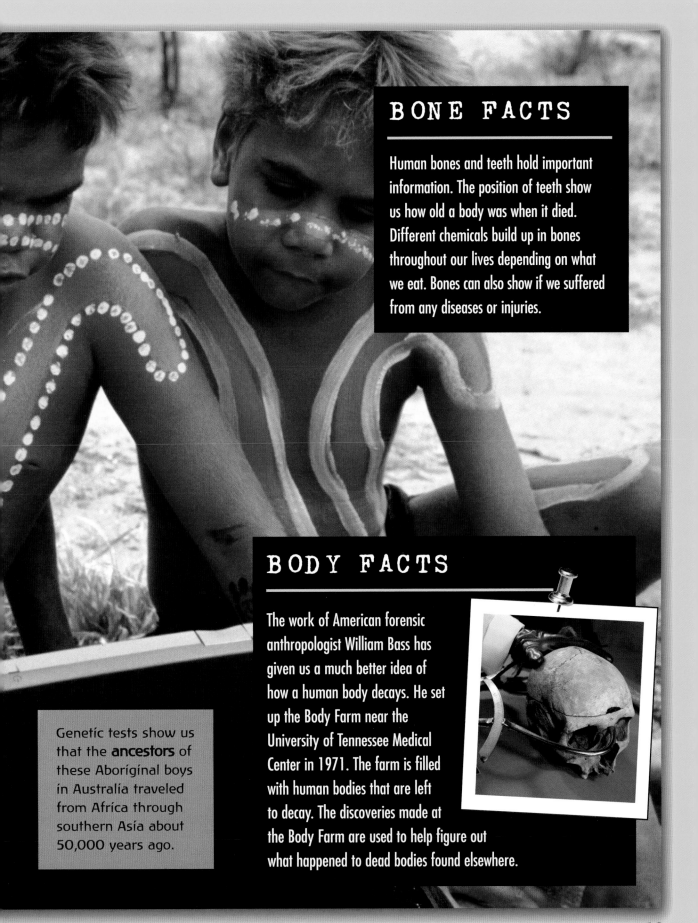

BONE FACTS

Human bones and teeth hold important information. The position of teeth show us how old a body was when it died. Different chemicals build up in bones throughout our lives depending on what we eat. Bones can also show if we suffered from any diseases or injuries.

BODY FACTS

The work of American forensic anthropologist William Bass has given us a much better idea of how a human body decays. He set up the Body Farm near the University of Tennessee Medical Center in 1971. The farm is filled with human bodies that are left to decay. The discoveries made at the Body Farm are used to help figure out what happened to dead bodies found elsewhere.

Genetic tests show us that the **ancestors** of these Aboriginal boys in Australia traveled from Africa through southern Asia about 50,000 years ago.

In 1993, the body of a 2,400-year-old woman was found in Russia. She was buried with a horse, which had maggots in its stomach. Scientists know that these maggots hatch in summer, so the ancient funeral must have been at that time of year.

DIET DISCOVERY

In the 1950s scientist discovered the body of a woman buried under the house of a wealthy Dutch family living in South Africa, in the 1700s. Studying her bones and teeth showed that until her 20s, the woman's diet was mainly grain. After that she ate seafood. At the time, seafood was a very inexpensive food—and fed mainly to slaves. This shows us that the woman became a slave as a young woman and died about 30 years later.

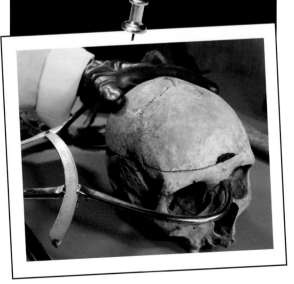

BURIED BONES

Anthropologists have been able to solve mysteries by simply examining the bones. Modern mysteries usually involve identifying a dead body and figuring out how they died. Forensic anthropologists are often asked to investigate **mass graves** where a **massacre** has taken place.

MAKING A FACE

When investigators cannot identify a dead body, they may turn to a forensic artist. Forensic artists study the shape of bones, especially the skull, to figure out what the living person would have looked like. One method is to measure the shape of the skull and use that to produce a drawing. The other way of doing it is to make a copy of the skull and add layers of muscles until it looks like a person (below). This process works just as well with ancient remains. It has been used so we can look into the eyes of famous mummies, such as Egypt's King Tutankhamun.

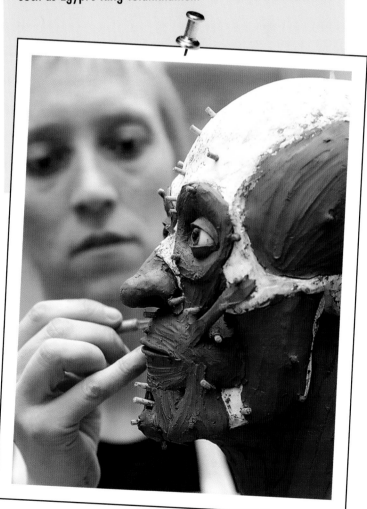

TIME CAPSULE

An anthropologist can figure out a person's age and sex just by looking at bones. An adult human has 206 bones but we are born with about 300. As we grow the bones slowly **fuse** together giving an indication of our age. The shapes and lengths of certain bones are different in female bodies compared to male ones.

RELATIONS

People have used many methods to trace the migration routes taken by humans as they spread around the world. Genetic testing is the most powerful tool. It shows who is most closely related to who and can be used to find the ancestors of the world's different races and groups.

Genetic tests show us that human beings evolved from an ape species about eight million years ago. However, we still share most of our **genes** with other large apes, such as chimpanzees and gorillas.

HOME AND AWAY

Scientists have traced back the origin of the human species to Africa. Experts have now mapped human movements over the last 50,000 years, as people spread to all **continents**.

Throughout human history, people have rarely traveled far from their birthplaces. Even today, most people spend their whole lives in one place. It is possible to pinpoint almost exactly where an ancient person was born by comparing his or her genes to those of living people. These tests show that an ancient mummy's relatives could still be living in the area thousands of years later.

These houses were built to the same design used in the Iron Age. Anthropologists live in the houses like Iron-Age people to learn more about their ancient **society**.

FOUND IN ICE

In 1991, the mummified remains of Ötzi (below) were discovered in the Alps, a mountain range in Europe. His body had been preserved for 5,300 years by snow and ice. Chemicals in his teeth showed that Ötzi had grown up near the modern village of Velturno, Italy. He died miles from home, perhaps killed during a raid on a neighboring tribe.

SET IN STONE

Ancient remains allow us to learn about how our own species evolved, and how the animals and plants alive today are different from those that lived in the past.

Stone objects can last for millions of years. Ancient stone tools, such as axes and arrowheads, are some of the few artifacts that remain from the earliest days of human history. A natural process can turn the remains of living things into stone. These **fossils** form a record of the history of life on Earth.

HUMAN FOSSILS

In 1997 a team of scientists found three human skulls in Ethiopia, Africa. There were also a number of stone tools. These fossils are 160,000 years old and are the earliest human beings ever found. The skulls were broken into many pieces. It took five years to put them back together.

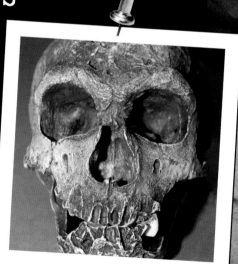

THE MISSING LINK

The fossil record of **hominids** is not complete. There is a lot we still do not know about how our species came into being. Some have suggested that there is an undiscovered species—the Missing Link—that would explain how we evolved from apes. Several times people have announced that they have found fossils of the Missing Link, but they have always been fakes with human bones mixed with those of other apes.

HUMAN TIMELINE

The first humans lived in Africa. They did not grow food, but had to hunt animals or gather wild plants to eat. Around 50,000 years ago people moved out of Africa for the first time. By 13,000 B.C rice was being farmed in Korea. By 10,000 B.C. people had spread across most of Earth's land. By 4500 B.C. **agriculture** had spread throughout the world.

Fossils are the only way we can study long **extinct** animals, such as dinosaurs.

STONE DEAD

Scientists who investigate fossils are called **paleontologists**. They are not just looking for old bones; they are interested in any evidence left by a living thing long ago. For example, the footprints left in the soft mud of a riverbank by a giant dinosaur.

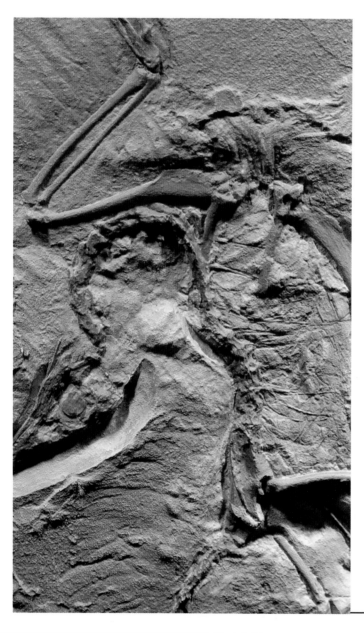

There are many places that you can go to find fossils. Fossil sites often have loose rocks and may be dangerous. Do not take risks to find a fossil. Look for field groups led by trained professionals. Museums have a lot of fossil displays and run programs so you can learn how to find fossils and figure out what they are and how old they are.

Some of the most famous fossils are of *Archaeopteryx*. This was one of the first species of bird and evolved from dinosaurs about 150 million years ago.

Millions of years later, a paleontologist can use the footprints to figure out how the dinosaur walked, how heavy it was, and how fast it could move. Paleontologists even study a dinosaur's fossilized droppings!

ON THE LEVEL

A fossil is always the same age as the rock in which it is found. Rocks are often formed in layers called **strata**. Strata that are buried deep underground are usually older than the ones located nearer to the surface. Paleontologists know that rocks found in different places are about the same age if they have the same types of fossil in them.

> Fossilized dinosaur footprints tell scientists how the animal walked and how fast they could run!

HOW DO FOSSILS FORM?

For a dead body to become a fossil, it must be protected in some way from damage. Normally it is buried in **sediment**, such as sand or mud. This process is most likely to happen if the body has been covered in water in some way. Water trickling through the sediment contains **minerals**. These gradually take the place of the chemicals in the dead creature. Over thousands of years, this process turns the body into solid rock. Fossils normally only show the hardest body parts, such as bones.

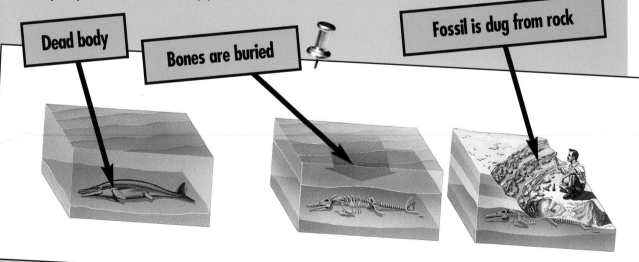

Dead body

Bones are buried

Fossil is dug from rock

CAVE DRAWINGS

Prehistoric humans left some **evidence** behind on purpose—cave drawings. The Rouffignac Cave in France has drawings in it that are about 15,000 years old. They are the oldest works of art in the world. The pictures are drawn with charcoal. Cave drawings often show wild animals, including detailed pictures of woolly **mammoths**. Mammoths are now extinct but they were hunted by prehistoric people.

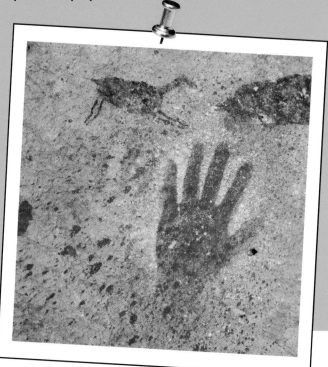

FAKE FACTS

For nearly 40 years in the first half of the 20th century, anthropologists believed that humans had evolved from Piltdown Man. A fossil of his broken skull had been dug up in England in 1912 by Charles Dawson. However, many experts were suspicious of the fossil. In 1953, it was proved that the Piltdown Man fossil had the skull bone of a human, but the jaw of an orangutan—an ape from Southeast Asia.

The tiny skull of Flores Man sits next to the head of a modern adult human. The small species has been nicknamed "The Hobbit."

BIG FAMILY

Anthropologists have discovered that human evolution is complicated. There have been several hominid species in the past. Many of them lived at the same time, but only our species, *Homo sapiens*, survives today. Our last surviving relative was Flores Man. This species was discovered in Indonesia in 2003. The fossils are tiny. Even adults only grew to 3 feet (1 m tall). The last Flores Man died 12,000 years ago.

THE LEAKEYS

Members of the Leakey family have been investigating human **origins** in Africa for 50 years. In 1959, Mary and Louis Leakey found the bones of hominids at Olduvai Gorge in Tanzania. Some of these fossils were ape-like animals that were 14 million years old. The couple's son, Richard, later found the bones of *Homo habilis* in Kenya (pictured). *Homo habilis* species lived about two million years ago. Its scientific name means "handy man" because its bones are often found with stone tools.

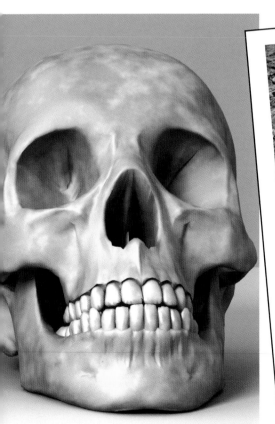

GLOSSARY

aerial To do with being in the air

agriculture The systems used to grow food

atoms The smallest parts of all substances

analyze Investigate using science

ancestors Your relatives that lived in the past

anthropologists Scientists who study how people live now and in the past

aqualungs Air tanks used by divers

archaeologists Scientists who search for ancient objects

artifacts Ancient objects created by people

cairns Piles of rocks made by people

continents The large land areas of the world, such as Africa, Asia, and North America

cultures The ways of life of different people around the world

decayed Broken down as an object got old

diets Foods people eat

evidence Clues that show what happened in the past

extinct When all members of a species have died out

forensic To do with solving crimes using science

fossils The remains of dead animals and plants that have turned to stone

fuse Join together so two things become one

genes The instructions that control how a body grows

genetic To do with genes, the instructions that control how a living body develops

hominids Extinct relatives of modern humans

Iron Age A time in the past when people learned to make iron tools

mammoths Hairy relatives of elephants that lived until a few thousand years ago

massacre When many people are murdered at the same time

mass graves A large grave filled with the bodies of many people

midden An ancient garbage dump

Middle Ages A period of history running from the 5th century to the 15th century

migration Long journeys made by people and other animals to find a good place to live

minerals Simple chemicals found in the environment

mummified Made into a mummy, a body that does not decay

Nobel Prize The top award in science, writing, and politics

origins Where things have come from

paleontologists Scientists that study fossils

papyrus A tough paper made from reeds

peat bogs Soggy swamps containing thick mud made from rotted wood

prehistoric Before history was recorded by people

preserved Remained undamaged

radar A way of making pictures with radio waves

radioactive Substances made up of atoms that fall apart and release radiation

sediment Sand, mud, and silt that settles to the bottom of rivers and oceans

society An organized group of people

strata Layers of different type of rock found under the ground

submersibles Small submarines

technology When science is used to make something useful

tombs Graves or buildings where dead bodies are placed

X-ray To examine something using radiation

FURTHER INFORMATION

Books

Archaeologists: Life Digging Up Artifacts by Holly Cefrey. New York, NY: Rosen Central, 2004.

Archaeology by Trevor Barnes. Boston, MA: Kingfisher, 2004.

Digging Up History: Archaeologists by Judy Monroe Peterson. New York, NY: PowerKids Press, 2009.

Dinosaur Dig by Dougal Dixon. Milwaukee, WI: Gareth Stevens Publishing, 2004.

History Detectives: Archaeologists by Richard and Louise Spilsbury. Chicago, IL: Heinemann Library, 2008.

Websites

Atlas of the Human Journey
https://www3.nationalgeographic.com/genographic/atlas.html

British Museum Collections
http://www.britishmuseum.org/the_museum/departments.aspx

Human Origins Program at the Smithsonian Institution:
http://anthropology.si.edu/humanorigins

Fossil Collecting 101
http://www.collectingfossils.org/fossilcollecting101.htm

Kon-Tiki Museum
http://www.kon-tiki.no/Ny/Dok_eng/e_start.html

INDEX